# Preach the Word

# Word

## Volume 7

Dr. Ricky Gravley

Word of His Mouth Publishers
Mooresboro, NC

All Scripture quotations are taken from the **King James Version** of the Bible.

ISBN: 978-1-941039-86-1
Printed in the United of the States of America
© 2016 by Dr. Ricky Gravley

Word of His Mouth Publishers
Mooresboro, NC
www.wordofhismouth.com

# Table of Contents

# "The Mother of Christ's Birth"
### Sermon #151

Text: Luke 1:26-38

**26** *And in the sixth month the angel Gabriel was sent from God unto a city of Galilee, named Nazareth,* **27** *To a virgin espoused to a man whose name was Joseph, of the house of David; and the virgin's name was Mary.* **28** *And the angel came in unto her, and said, Hail, thou that art highly favoured, the Lord is with thee: blessed art thou among women.* **29** *And when she saw him, she was troubled at his saying, and cast in her mind what manner of salutation this should be.* **30** *And the angel said unto her, Fear not, Mary: for thou hast found favour with God.* **31** *And, behold, thou shalt conceive in thy womb, and bring forth a son, and shalt call his name JESUS.* **32** *He shall be great, and shall be called the Son of the Highest: and the Lord God shall give unto him the throne of his father David:* **33** *And he shall reign over the house of Jacob for ever; and of his kingdom there shall be no end.* **34** *Then said Mary unto the angel, How shall this be, seeing I know not a man?* **35** *And the angel answered and said unto her, The Holy Ghost shall come upon thee, and the power of the Highest shall overshadow thee: therefore also that holy thing which shall be born of thee shall be called the Son of God.* **36** *And, behold, thy cousin Elisabeth, she hath also conceived a son in her old age: and this is the sixth month with her, who was called barren.* **37** *For with God nothing shall be impossible.* **38** *And Mary said, Behold the handmaid of the Lord; be it unto me according to thy word. And the angel departed from her.*

<u>Intro:</u>
## Note with me three important points within our text
vs. 26.............. We see the visitor. (Angel Gabriel)
vs. 27...... We see the virgin. (2 times word virgin)
vs. 28-38.............................. We see the visitation.
The visitation is to Mary, but it's not about Mary, it's about Jesus. However, Mary plays a vital role in God's plan. She's the instrument that God chose to use to bring Christ into this world. **(Title)** Look closely at the visitation that takes place between Gabriel and Mary.

Seven truths in this text.

| | |
|---|---|
| vs. 28 | Mary's salutation. |
| vs. 29 | Mary's surprise. (Seemed like any other day.) |
| vs. 30 | Mary's standing. (Why was she chosen? Grace) |
| vs. 31-33 | Mary's son. |
| vs. 34 | Mary's skepticism. (Does not understand his plan.) |
| vs. 35-37 | Mary's security. |
| vs. 38 | Mary's submission. (Fully submits to God's will.) |

## 5 truths we know about Mary according to scripture
1. Mary was holy ............................................. vs. 27
   (Not sinless but pure morally)
2. Mary was honored ......................................... vs. 28
   (God had chosen to bless her)
3. Mary was human........................................... vs. 30
   (She was not a wonder woman)
4. Mary was happy........................................vs. 46-47
   (Serving Him with gladness)

5.  Mary was humble............................................. vs. 48
    (God always uses the humble)

I want us to look this morning at how the announcement
of Christ's birth affected the mother of Jesus.

## I.  The announcement of His birth taught her
   A.  She learned of His person ..................... vs. 31
   B.  She learned of His promise .................. vs. 32
   C.  She learned of His position .................. vs. 32
   D.  She learned of His power ..................... vs. 32
   E.  She learned of His permanency ........... vs. 33

## II.  The announcement of His birth tested her
   A.  Her fiancé questioned her ............. Matt. 1:21
   B.  Her family questioned her.
   C.  Her friends questioned her.

If a young woman was accused of adultery, even in
betrothal period, she was to be taken to the priest, and
investigation would take place. If she was found guilty,
her husband could divorce her or have her stoned, with
him casting the first stone followed by the entire
community stoning her to death.

## III.  The announcement of His birth transformed her
   She would no longer be the same after this
   visitation.
   A.  She faced fear........................................ vs. 30
   B.  She found favor..................................... vs. 30
   C.  She flourished in faith..................... vs. 37-38

(She simply chose to believe God in spite of what others might say or think.)

**_Conclusion:_** Most all commentators believe Mary was a teenager when Gabriel appeared unto her. What courage this young teen girl displayed, once she learned of His birth, believed His birth, then boldly told of His birth to others, not fearing the consequences that could come.

# "The Miracle of Christ's Birth"
### Sermon #152

Text: Matthew 1:18-25

**18** *Now the birth of Jesus Christ was on this wise: When as his mother Mary was espoused to Joseph, before they came together, she was found with child of the Holy Ghost.* **19** *Then Joseph her husband, being a just man, and not willing to make her a publick example, was minded to put her away privily.* **20** *But while he thought on these things, behold, the angel of the Lord appeared unto him in a dream, saying, Joseph, thou son of David, fear not to take unto thee Mary thy wife: for that which is conceived in her is of the Holy Ghost.* **21** *And she shall bring forth a son, and thou shalt call his name JESUS: for he shall save his people from their sins.* **22** *Now all this was done, that it might be fulfilled which was spoken of the Lord by the prophet, saying,* **23** *Behold, a virgin shall be with child, and shall bring forth a son, and they shall call his name Emmanuel, which being interpreted is, God with us.* **24** *Then Joseph being raised from sleep did as the angel of the Lord had bidden him, and took unto him his wife:* **25** *And knew her not till she had brought forth her firstborn son: and he called his name JESUS.*

Intro: The passage this morning reflected on Mary, and the passage tonight reflects on Joseph. Again I want to emphasize that this passage also is not about Joseph, but it's about Jesus. However, Joseph certainly deserves to be recognized for the Scripture recognizes him.

1.   Joseph's ignorance .......................................... vs. 18
     This is not a miracle to him at this point; it's a mess.
     He does not see nor believe what is happening. He,
     no doubt, wanted to believe Mary, but how could
     he? It just doesn't seem possible.

2.   Joseph's intentions .......................................... vs. 19
     He does not want to hurt Mary nor does he desire
     to humiliate her, so he is contemplating on
     terminating the marriage.

3.   Joseph's instructions ...................................... vs. 20
     He also has a visitation from another world. The
     angel declares that Mary is telling the truth and
     instructs him to take her as his wife.
     Note that Joseph:
     Fears the engagement ...................................... vs. 18
     Feels the embarrassment .............................. vs. 19
     Finds the encouragement ............................. vs. 20

What's amazing to me is that both Joseph and Mary were
willing to suffer their character and their reputation to
believe the promise of God and witness the miracle of
Christ's birth. **(Title)**

I.   **The prophecy of this miracle - vs. 21**
     A.   The nature of it was prophesied, "she shall
          bring forth a son."
     B.   The name was prophesied, "call his name
          Jesus."
     C.   The need of it was prophesied, "to save his
          people."

## II.	The purpose of this miracle - vs. 22
    A.	Because of the completion of the Bible .........
    ..................................................... vs. 22, Is. 7:14
    B.	Because of the corruption of blood ...............
    ........................................................Rom. 5:12
    Christ had the flesh of a woman, but the blood of God!

## Proof that His blood was not man's blood.
1.	Eph. 1:7 ........His blood gives us redemption.
2.	Col. 1:14...... His blood gives us forgiveness.
3.	Rom. 5:9.......His blood saves us from wrath.
4.	1 Jn. 1:9.......His blood cleanses us from all sins.
5.	Matt. 27:4.....His blood is declared to be innocent.
6.	1 Peter 1:19 .. His blood is declared precious.
7.	Acts 20:28 .. His blood purchased the church.
8.	Rev. 12:11 ....... His blood gives men victory.

## III.	The proof of this miracle - vs. 24-25
    A.	The proof is in the Word ...................... vs. 22
    B.	The proof is in the womb ..................... vs. 23
    C.	The proof is in the witnesses...........vs. 24-25 (Joseph)

## Think about people who witnessed and declared His birth.
1.	The angels declared it ................Matt. 1-2, Lu. 1-2
2.	Mary declared it ...................................Lu. 1:28-56
3.	Elizabeth declared it............................Lu. 1:39-45
4.	John the Baptist witnessed it..................... Lu. 1:41

# "The Moment of Christ's Birth"
## Sermon #153

Text: Luke 2:1-7

**1** *And it came to pass in those days, that there went out a decree from Cæsar Augustus, that all the world should be taxed.* **2** *(And this taxing was first made when Cyrenius was governor of Syria.)* **3** *And all went to be taxed, every one into his own city.* **4** *And Joseph also went up from Galilee, out of the city of Nazareth, into Judæa, unto the city of David, which is called Bethlehem; (because he was of the house and lineage of David:)* **5** *To be taxed with Mary his espoused wife, being great with child.* **6** *And so it was, that, while they were there, the days were accomplished that she should be delivered.* **7** *And she brought forth her firstborn son, and wrapped him in swaddling clothes, and laid him in a manger; because there was no room for them in the inn.*

Intro: As we look at this passage this morning, keep in mind that Luke places special emphasis on three things surrounding Christ's birth.

1.    He emphasizes the taxation...........................vs. 1-5
2.    He emphasizes the traveling ...........................vs. 4
3.    He emphasizes the trough...............................vs. 7

That's what a manger was, a stone trough that had been carved out for the feeding of animals. We will say more about that in the message. **(Title)**

## I. The taxation (the providence that surrounded them) - vs.1

God was working and orchestrating the events around them. Caesar Augustus was the favored grandnephew of Julius Caesar. After the murder of Julius Caesar and the suicide of his great rival (Mark Anthony) Caesar Augustus steps on the scene. Now every 14 years Rome would call for a census for both military and tax purposes. At that time every Jewish male was required to return to the city of his father and record his name, occupation, property, and family. (What does this have to do with Christ's birth?) It's been around 9 months since the angel visited Joseph and Mary. They're living in Galilee in the city of Nazareth. Micah the prophet (5:2) prophesied some 600 - 700 years earlier that Christ would be born in Bethlehem. God was working to get Joseph and Mary out of Nazareth to Bethlehem. Proof of this providence is in verse 2. This taxation didn't even go in effect for ten more years when Cyrenius became governor of Syria. Christ was 10 years old when this went in effect. (Why did God do all this? Because Jesus could not have the blood of man flowing in his veins. He had the flesh of a woman but the blood of God. But to sit on the throne of David his genealogy had to come from his father. Christ was conceived of the Holy Ghost, born of a virgin woman, had the flesh of humanity but not the blood of humanity, and because his earthly father was of the house and lineage of David, (vs.4) it therefore qualified him to sit upon the throne.

## II.    The traveling (the problems that surrounded them) - vs. 5-6

According to verse five Joseph and Mary are still engaged. Engagements or betrothals were so serious that they were considered and called wives even at this point. But note the problems they encounter on their journey.

A    The mother's condition was a problem.. vs. 6
   She's nine months pregnant; she's not fit to be traveling. This was at least a three day's journey to Jerusalem then another 5 to 6 more miles to Bethlehem.

B.    The masses in the city were a problem.
   When Joseph finally gets to Bethlehem, the city is overrun with masses of people. They have all come in to town for the same reason. Can you imagine, they are already exhausted, and now they have to fight the crowd to find a place to rest.

C.    The motel accommodations were a problem vs. 7
   There's a "No Vacancy" sign out front on every inn. They are forced to stay in the stable among the animals of those who have already found lodging for the night. No doubt the stables were as full as the inns. Most historians record that stables in Bible days were often caves that had been formed and used for the animals. (Picture the scene of Joseph and Mary and Jesus.)

### III. The trough (the poverty that surrounded them) - vs. 7

The manger was normally 3 feet tall, 2 feet wide, and 3 to 4 feet in length. It was a large piece of stone that had been carved out into a trough that was used to feed and water animals. This speaks of the great depth of poverty that Christ plummeted to, in order to rescue man. (2 Cor. 8:9)

**Notice three truths about the manger.**

A. The manger was a type .......................... vs. 7
I understand that the manger was an object and not a person, but it still reminds me in many ways of a sinner.

   1   It was lifeless ..................... Eph. 2:1-10
   2.   It was filthy (All of our righteousness is filthy rags.)
   3.   It was cold and hard (like every sinner)
   4.   It was empty (They didn't lay Christ in a manger that was full; it was empty. Every sinner is empty inside; there is a void that only Christ can fill.)
   5.   It was insignificant (The only reason why it was in the Bible was because Jesus was put into it. There was nothing special about the manger, it was what was placed inside of it that made it special. Same is true about us.)
   6.   The bread of life was placed in it!

B. The manger was a tool .......................... vs. 7
God used an earthen vessel, that is what a manger is, an earthen vessel to carry substance to the needs of others. That's what

15

we are just earthen vessels that God can use to carry the gospel. In this manger laid the gospel, and inside of us the treasure we have is the gospel.

C.   The manger was a testimony..........vs. 12, 16
    1.     It revealed Christ poverty.
    2.     It revealed Christ person.............vs. 16

# "The Messengers of Christ's Birth"
## Sermon #154

Text: Luke 2:8-20

**8** *And there were in the same country shepherds abiding in the field, keeping watch over their flock by night.* **9** *And, lo, the angel of the Lord came upon them, and the glory of the Lord shone round about them: and they were sore afraid.* **10** *And the angel said unto them, Fear not: for, behold, I bring you good tidings of great joy, which shall be to all people.* **11** *For unto you is born this day in the city of David a Saviour, which is Christ the Lord.* **12** *And this shall be a sign unto you; Ye shall find the babe wrapped in swaddling clothes, lying in a manger.* **13** *And suddenly there was with the angel a multitude of the heavenly host praising God, and saying,* **14** *Glory to God in the highest, and on earth peace, good will toward men.* **15** *And it came to pass, as the angels were gone away from them into heaven, the shepherds said one to another, Let us now go even unto Bethlehem, and see this thing which is come to pass, which the Lord hath made known unto us.* **16** *And they came with haste, and found Mary, and Joseph, and the babe lying in a manger.* **17** *And when they had seen it, they made known abroad the saying which was told them concerning this child.* **18** *And all they that heard it wondered at those things which were told them by the shepherds.* **19** *But Mary kept all these things, and pondered them in her heart.* **20** *And the shepherds returned, glorifying and praising God for all the things that they had heard and seen, as it was told unto them.*

Intro: If we look at this passage as a whole we see two different evangelistic groups. Both of whom had the privilege of announcing that the Savior of this world had been born. One group announces His birth to the other, then they take the message and carry to others who have not heard. That is exactly how the gospel works. You will also note that the first group of messengers is heavenly, while the other group is earthly. **(Title)**

## Six things Luke mentions in this passage:

1.  The shepherds ................................................. vs. 8
2.  The Shekinah glory ........................................ vs. 9
3.  The salvation................................................ vs. 10
    (good tidings - the gospel)
4.  The Savior..................................................... vs. 11
5.  The sign..................................................... vs. 12, 16
6.  The singing ............................................... vs. 13-14

## Note that in vs. 14 that this is no ordinary song. This is no ordinary song because it doesn't have an ordinary message.

1.  Song of God's praise "Glory to God in the Highest."
2.  Song of God's peace "and on earth peace"
3.  Song of God's purpose "good will toward men"
    The angels were the 1$^{st}$ to announce the Savior's birth and the Shepherds were the 2$^{nd}$.

How was the message first presented?

1.  It was a glorious message ............................... vs. 9
2.  It was a good message .................................. vs. 10
3.  It was a glad message.................................... vs. 10

4.    It was a gospel message ..............................vs. 11

What is so amazing is not only how this message was first announced, but to whom it was first announced. It was announced to shepherds. Shepherds to the world were looked down upon. They were seen as dirty, despised, and dumb men, men of ignorant and low degree. Shepherds were never permitted in a court of law. Ivor Powel said that often times when there were no wild beasts in the area, when thieves were not prevalent, the shepherding of sheep was entrusted to children. Society often looked at these men as doing the work of children. In other words, if you cared for sheep, then you were seen as unfit for greater tasks. This raises a question in my mind, why then did the message of the Savior's birth come to these men first? Why not a king, or a priest, or some religious sector of the day?

I.    **Because of the place they stood - vs. 8 "in the same country"**
They were close to where He was. God always uses those who are close to His son. Also the Bible says they were, "abiding in the field...". The field is a type of the world. God has always had an interest in the world. This is why Jesus came into the world. Jesus told us to lift up our eyes and look on the field...(Jn.4:35)

II.   **Because of the profession they shared - vs. 8 "shepherds"**
John the Baptist announced Christ to be the Lamb of God. In John 10 He is the good shepherd, He is

19

also seen in the Bible as the great shepherd and the chief shepherd. No doubt David said it best when he declared Him to be "My shepherd". It only makes sense that He would first have His birth to be announced to shepherds.

### III.   Because of the period - vs. 8 "over their flock by night"

One practical reason, is because they were probably the only ones awake. Shepherds were required to sit up through the night to watch for wild beasts that may try to come and steal the sheep. It's very possible that they were the only ones awake. It pays to spend secret time with God.

### IV.   Because of the poverty - vs. 8

It's no secret that shepherds were oftentimes the poorest of men. We saw how poor Christ became in vs. 7. Born in a stable, with no place to call His own. Again 2 Cor. 8:9 comes to my mind. Christ was not born into royalty but poverty, therefore, He shared the message first with those who were of like status.

### What do we learn from this other group of messengers?

1. They were watching .......................................... vs. 8
2. They were worried ............................................ vs. 9
3. They were wondering ............................... vs. 10-14
   (stood in amazement)
4. They were willing .................................... vs. 15-16
   (left all behind)

5.  They were worshiping ............................vs. 17-18

**_Conclusion:_** The gospel message has always been "come and see and go and tell." The shepherds were excited to hear the message of His birth, excited to see the Savior, and excited to share with others what they had both heard and witnessed. So should we that are saved. We are God's messengers, and we should be just as excited to share the gospel with others.

# "The Magi at Christ's Birth"
## Sermon #155

Text: Matt. 2:1-12

**1** *Now when Jesus was born in Bethlehem of Judaea in the days of Herod the king, behold, there came wise men from the east to Jerusalem,* **2** *Saying, Where is he that is born King of the Jews? for we have seen his star in the east, and are come to worship him.* **3** *When Herod the king had heard these things, he was troubled, and all Jerusalem with him.* **4** *And when he had gathered all the chief priests and scribes of the people together, he demanded of them where Christ should be born.* **5** *And they said unto him, In Bethlehem of Judaea: for thus it is written by the prophet,* **6** *And thou Bethlehem, in the land of Juda, art not the least among the princes of Juda: for out of thee shall come a Governor, that shall rule my people Israel.* **7** *Then Herod, when he had privily called the wise men, enquired of them diligently what time the star appeared.* **8** *And he sent them to Bethlehem, and said, Go and search diligently for the young child; and when ye have found him, bring me word again, that I may come and worship him also.* **9** *When they had heard the king, they departed; and, lo, the star, which they saw in the east, went before them, till it came and stood over where the young child was.* **10** *When they saw the star, they rejoiced with exceeding great joy.* **11** *And when they were come into the house, they saw the young child with Mary his mother, and fell down, and worshipped him: and when they had opened their treasures, they presented unto him gifts; gold, and frankincense, and myrrh.* **12** *And being warned of God in a dream that they*

*should not return to Herod, they departed into their own*
*country another way.*

Intro: The Chaldeans had been stargazers since they were children. They studied the stars on a nightly basis. God used angels to speak to the shepherds because they studied angels, and He used stars to speak to these men because they studied stars. The Lord knows what to use and when to use something or someone to speak to men where they are.

1.  The person born is Jesus .................................... vs. 1
2.  The place is Bethlehem of Judea .................... vs. 1
3.  The people who are bound for Jerusalem ....... vs. 1

1.  Their request to see the King ......................... vs. 2
2.  Their revelation to go see this King .............. vs. 2
3.  Their reason to see the King .......................... vs. 2

I am interested in both the witness and the worship of these wise men. The reason is because the Bible places a lot of emphasis on these two subjects in this passage of Scripture.

**I.  <u>The witness of these wise men - vs. 2</u>**
    For these men it all started with a star! The star is what led them to the Savior!
    1.  The trusting of the star ......................... vs. 2
    2.  The telling about the star........................ vs. 2
    3.  The timing of this star ........................... vs. 7
    4.  The traveling of this star ....................... vs. 9
    5.  The thankfulness for the star................ vs. 10

23

    1.    This star was seen ................................. vs. 2
    2.    This star was shared ............................. vs. 2
    3.    This star was special ............................ vs. 2
        (it was His star)

## II.   The worship of these wise men - vs. 2, 7-12
    A.   I see their guide to worship .................... vs. 2
    B.   I see their gladness to worship .............. vs. 2
    C.   I see their gifts in worship ..................... vs. 2

### It's also important to note:
    1.    Their anticipation to worship ................ vs. 2
    2.    Their adversary of worship ................. vs. 7-8
    3.    Their action of worship ..................... vs. 9-11
    4.    Their admonition after worship ........... vs. 12

Worship always came with a price tag in the Scriptures. In fact, the saints in the Scripture did not really call it true worship, if it did not cost them something.

## III.  The wisdom of these wise men - vs. 2-12
    A.   They were looking for God .................... vs. 2
    B.   They were longing for God ................. vs. 8-9
    C.   They were listening to God ................. vs. 12

***Conclusion:*** The truth is that wise men still follow Jesus!

# "The Pool of Mercy"
## Sermon #156

Text: John 5:1-4

**1** *After this there was a feast of the Jews; and Jesus went up to Jerusalem.* **2** *Now there is at Jerusalem by the sheep market a pool, which is called in the Hebrew tongue Bethesda, having five porches.* **3** *In these lay a great multitude of impotent folk, of blind, halt, withered, waiting for the moving of the water.* **4** *For an angel went down at a certain season into the pool, and troubled the water: whosoever then first after the troubling of the water stepped in was made whole of whatsoever disease he had.*

Intro: I have purposely left off the main emphasis of this miracle to look at the early verse recorded. I plan to address those verses in another sermon at another time. **(Title)**

1.     **The feast of the Jews - vs. 1**
       We won't take the time to debate what feast the Bible is talking about in our text. Some believe this feast to be the feast of Pentecost, some 50 days after the Passover. Others believe it to be the feast of Purim and some believe it to be the feast of Tabernacles. It really is not worth debating. The Bible just says, ***"After this there was a feast of the Jews"***.

**2.    The footsteps of Jesus - vs. 1**

No matter what feast it was, Jesus saw the importance of being there. The Bible says, *"and Jesus went up to Jerusalem."* This feast brought those who desired to worship and the opportunity for Christ to bring His message to such a large crowd. This alone may have been the very reason Christ was present at this occasion. However, I want us to follow the footsteps of our Savior up to Jerusalem to this feast.

**3.    The fountain at Jerusalem - vs. 2**

The sheep market or gate mentioned here was the entrance that Nehemiah had built in Neh. 3:1 in the restoration of the city. It was of great importance because it is where the animals would enter for sacrifice. I can see the Lamb of God walking through the sheep gate toward the temple.

Once you entered through that gate toward the temple you would see this pool and these five porches. Some believe those to have been arches or entrances in one pentagonal building and at the center was this famous pool called *Bethesda. Bethesda means: "House of mercy or compassion".*

**Three truths concerning this pool of mercy.**

**I.    The multitude around the pool - vs. 3**

    A.    The size of this multitude. "great"

    B.    The sickness of this multitude.

    C.    The seriousness of this multitude.

These people are weak, wanting, willing, and waiting for one thing: "the moving of the water". Are we? Their desperate need was what kept and held them there. Are we willing to wait for God to move and stir the waters in our hearts and lives to see the need met?

## II. The miracle in the pool - vs. 4
    A.    This was supernatural. "an angel"
    B.    This was seasonal. "at a certain season"
    C.    This was a stirring. "troubled the waters"
        This was not an act of man but was an act of God. God was moving in the midst of these folks. This moving of the waters was a sovereign act of God. We need God to trouble the waters of our hearts and move in power in our lives like He has in the past.

## III. The message from the pool - vs. 4
The big question that comes to mind is why did God do this? We don't always understand the mind of God and God doesn't always give us an explanation as to why He chooses to do something. He doesn't owe us one either, by the way. We are also aware of the fact that God doesn't do anything without a purpose.
    A.    The spiritual formalism
        They had a temple, priests, worship, sacrifices, and a congregation, but it meant nothing to them. Every church should be a house of mercy or a house of compassion.

The temple had become everything but a house of mercy or compassion. The people that were the most needy were on the outside rather than on the inside.

B.   The silent factor
God hadn't spoken since the days of Malachi. The temple was hopeless and the priests were powerless.

God wasn't working on the inside; He was working on the outside. Just like in Rev. 3 He was on the outside because man would not let Him in.

C.   The strengthening of faith
Every time God stirred these waters and changed an individual, faith was stirred in the hearts of others. This moving of the waters caused others to believe that if God did it for them, then He could do it for me. Faith is always individual.

**_Conclusion_**: How long are you willing to wait for the moving of the waters? Do you long for Him to stir the waters of your soul? Will you be the first to get in? Those were the ones who got help. The ones who said, "I'm waiting Lord, no matter how long it takes; I am willing to be the first to get in!"

# "The Place of Misery"
## Sermon #157

Text: John 5:5-7

**5** *And a certain man was there, which had an infirmity thirty and eight years.* **6** *When Jesus saw him lie, and knew that he had been now a long time in that case, he saith unto him, Wilt thou be made whole?* **7** *The impotent man answered him, Sir, I have no man, when the water is troubled, to put me into the pool: but while I am coming, another steppeth down before me.*

Intro: I want us to see in this message how that this "pool of mercy" had become a "place of misery". One might think with all the miracles that had taken place at this pool, "How could this place ever become a place of misery?" Because as great as one miracle was it didn't help all who were in need. It left many wanting and waiting for another season. These five porches in vs. 4 represent the five books of Moses in the Old Testament. The law could not fulfill man's needs, it could only leave men wanting just like the pool. The people around this pool had nothing to look forward to outside this miracle other than the religious activity day in and day out. Israel had grown so deep in religion and so far from God that their priests were powerless and calloused toward even the weakest of society. God had not spoken to them in over 400 years. They had a form of godliness but they denied the power thereof. There was no one who knew it better than the man in our text. Just like the nation of Israel he had laid by this pool for years hoping to receive a miracle and had gotten nowhere. With a miracle pool on one side of him and temple worship on the other he was living in a place of misery. Why? Because it's not miracles and religion that people need. They need Christ! This man needed Christ! He represents every man!

**I.    <u>Notice the man - vs. 5</u>**
    A.    This was a certain man. (he was a real individual)
    B.    This was a church man. (he believed in miracles)
    C.    This was a crippled man. (infirmity)

**II.   <u>Notice the master - vs. 6</u>**
    A.    Jesus sees this man.
        "When Jesus saw him"
        He took notice of him when no one else did. I'm glad the Lord came looking for me.
    B.    Jesus sympathizes with this man.
        "knew he had been there a long time in that case"
    C.    Jesus speaks to this man.
        "Wilt thou be made whole?"
        Christ is bringing this man to the realization of where he is.

**III.  <u>Notice the misery - vs. 7</u>**
This is the point we want to emphasize.
    A.    This man was lonely. "Sir I have no man."
        Ps. 142:4 I looked on my right hand, and beheld, but there was no man that would know me: refuge failed me; no man cared for my soul.

B.   This man was lame. "to put me in the pool"
     He needed someone to lift him up out of the
     condition he was in and place him in the
     water. He could not help himself. (Rom. 3:10,
     23)
C.   This man was longing. "while I am coming"
     Even though he knew he would never be able
     to get in the waters he was trying with all his
     strength to get in! Just like religion, man will
     do his best to try, hoping that somehow or
     someway by some chance he might make it.
D.   This man was lost. "another steppeth down"
     He came up short every single time. He was
     miserable because he was lost. Someone
     always stood in his way. For thirty-eight
     years he sat here hoping for a change only to
     find himself still lost without hope. He gives
     us the testimony of every sinner who has
     never come to know Christ. They live in this
     place of misery.

**_Conclusion:_** Seeking after miracles will leave you just
like this man. He was helpless and hopeless when Jesus
found him. Religion didn't even come outside to try and
offer him any help. This man needed someone to help
him. He needed someone who cared. That is what every
sinner needs today is someone to care for their condition.
I'm glad that there is someone who cares and His name
is Jesus!

# "The Power of the Mighty"
Sermon #158

Text: John 5:8-9
**8** *Jesus saith unto him, Rise, take up thy bed, and walk.*
**9** *And immediately the man was made whole, and took up his bed, and walked: and on the same day was the sabbath.*

Intro: For thirty-eight years this man had been without hope. Trying to the best of his ability to find a miracle, he came up short each and every time. His only companions were others who were in need. The miracle crowd had left him and the religious crowd didn't want him. Today is a different day in his life for Jesus has passed by inquiring to him about his need. Christ is about to demonstrate and display his power in this man's life.

1.  Christ speaks to this man in a direct manner .. vs. 8
2.  Christ speaks to this man in a different manner... .......................................................... vs. 8
3.  Christ speaks to this man in a divine manner . vs. 8

This man's life is about to be forever changed. The mighty power of God is about to be manifested in his life! **(Title)**

**I.    The power of His might saved him - vs. 8**
   A.    From a life of sin.
         According to our Lord's conversation with this man in the temple he had lived a life of sin. (vs.14) This sin could very well have

32

been the reason for his infirmity. He now had a choice. He did not have to be in bondage to sin anymore. Christ had made him free from a life of sin.

B.    From a life of shame.

The shame of being a fully grown man and having to be carried around like a baby. To have to beg for the help and aid of others. No doubt he was filthy and vile because of his inability to get up to go to the restroom and clean and care for himself.

C.    From a life of sorrow.

Everyday tasks were constant struggles for him. Just to get through a normal day required so much more out of him. He lived a very sorrowful life.

## II.    <u>The power of His might sanctified him - vs. 8</u>

This power not only got him up, but it cleaned him up. This man had a resurrection but he also had a responsibility. His bed represented:

A.    His old life.

It carried the stains of his past. Jesus did not want it left there to be remembered or seen by others. There was nothing left of what he used to be. It was erased by the removal of his garment.

B.    His old look.

He was not that man anymore. Taking up his bed was something that he was used to doing. His bed went everywhere he went. This man could take up his bed for the last time. He no longer needed to carry it with him anymore. He was no longer dependent on it anymore. When you saw him at this point, you would see a different man on the outside. He had a new look.

## III.  <u>The power of His might stabilized him - vs. 8</u>
His legs were given back to him:
A.  For growth
This man was raised to walk in newness of life. Christ wanted him to use his new ability, not waste it. He was no longer to be dependent upon others but what Christ had done for him
B.  For going
He could now go places he could have never dreamed of. Christ will take each of us to new heights in life if we will go forward for His glory. It is both the desire and the will of God that we go forward in Christ.
C.  For glory
This man could glorify Christ by simply exercising the ability that God had blessed him with. His life was changed to glorify Christ. Those who knew him before could look at his life every day and see the change Christ had made in him. This alone would bring glory to God.


***Conclusion:*** Can people look at our life and see the power of Christ on us and in us? Can they see the

34

outward change of an inward change in our lives? Do they know that we have met the Master?

# "The Persecution of Men"
### Sermon #159

Text: John 5:10-16

**10** *The Jews therefore said unto him that was cured, It is the sabbath day: it is not lawful for thee to carry thy bed.* **11** *He answered them, He that made me whole, the same said unto me, Take up thy bed, and walk.* **12** *Then asked they him, What man is that which said unto thee, Take up thy bed, and walk?* **13** *And he that was healed wist not who it was: for Jesus had conveyed himself away, a multitude being in that place.* **14** *Afterward Jesus findeth him in the temple, and said unto him, Behold, thou art made whole: sin no more, lest a worse thing come unto thee.* **15** *The man departed, and told the Jews that it was Jesus, which had made him whole.* **16** *And therefore did the Jews persecute Jesus, and sought to slay him, because he had done these things on the sabbath day.*

Intro: Thus far we have seen a suffering patient, a sympathizing physician and now we will look at the scornful Pharisees. Like so many times in the gospels, the religious crowd was driven to anger by the display of God's power before them. Christ broke their religious rules and insulted their sinful pride. The end result was that it caused great opposition toward Him and those that follow Him. (vs.16) **(Title)**

## I.   The attack on the man - vs. 10-13
A.   They had no consideration for this man.
B.   They had no congratulation for this man.
C.   They had no celebration for this man.

If you think that this religious world is going to be happy because Christ found you, then you are badly mistaken. They turned on him because Christ had turned toward him. There is no clear indication in our text that this man ever received Christ as his Savior. However, we do find him in the temple perhaps thanking God for what had transpired in his life. This alone would have been enough to cause this crowd to attack him.

II. **The attack on the master - vs. 16**
    Notice what led up to this attack on Jesus.
    A.  The accusers............................................ vs. 10
        (The offended)
    B.  The answer............................................. vs. 11
        (The obedience)
    C.  The asking............................................. vs. 12
        (The observation)
    D.  The audience .......................................... vs. 13
        (The obscurity)
    E.  The afterward ......................................... vs. 14
        (The order)
    F.  The announcement ................................. vs. 15
        (The opportunity)
    G.  The aggression ....................................... vs. 16
        (The opposition)

III. **The attack on the ministry - vs. 16, 18**
    This religious crowd got so upset that they wanted to kill Jesus. (vs.16) They didn't like His <u>works</u> according to verse sixteen, and they didn't like His

word according to verse eighteen. The world's answer for Christianity today is to kill it out. (Muslims) True religion will shine its light on false religion. Christianity exposes false religion for what it really is, a lie. No matter how much Christ helped others, the religious world despised Him for this reason alone.

A.    We are to expect persecution ......2 Tim. 3:12
B.    We are to endure persecution.........................
        ...........................................Matt. 5:11-12, 44
C.    We are to be encouraged in persecution ........
        .........................................................Jn. 15:20

**_Conclusion:_** This passage of scripture proves the cruelty of religion. Religion hates anything and anyone to do with Christ. Religion seeks to kill out Christianity. Just as God uses men to bring men to Christ, Satan uses men to turn men from Christ. Christianity will turn you away from religious pride and religious pride will turn you away from Christianity.

# "Cain the Apostate"
## (The Way of Cain)
### Sermon #160

Text: Gen. 4:1-5

**1** *And Adam knew Eve his wife; and she conceived, and bare Cain, and said, I have gotten a man from the LORD.* **2** *And she again bare his brother Abel. And Abel was a keeper of sheep, but Cain was a tiller of the ground.* **3** *And in process of time it came to pass, that Cain brought of the fruit of the ground an offering unto the LORD.* **4** *And Abel, he also brought of the firstlings of his flock and of the fat thereof. And the LORD had respect unto Abel and to his offering:* **5** *But unto Cain and to his offering he had not respect. And Cain was very wroth, and his countenance fell.*

Intro:

**I.  Cain and his opportunity - vs. 1**
   A.  Cain was the first born.
   B.  Cain was the first boy.
       His mother thought he was the Christ! Cain was however more of an anti-Christ.
   C.  Cain was the first brother. (Big brother)

**II.  Cain and his occupation - vs. 2**
   A.  It involved gardening.
   B.  It involved growing.
   C.  It involved the ground.
       All three of these have something to do with the fall and sin. While Cain's garden was

growing, there were some things growing in his heart as well. (Pride, rebellion)

## III.  Cain and his offering - vs. 3-5
    A.   Cain's offering was rebellion .....He had light
    B.   Cain's offering was religious............ 1st false
    C.   Cain's offering was rejected ................... vs. 5

## *Why did God reject Cain's offering?*

## I.  He traded reason for revelation
Salvation is built upon three important facts.
    A.   The word of God.
    B.   The work of Christ.
    C.   The witness of the Spirit.
         Cain ignored all three of these. He sought redemption and peace with God his own way rather than God's way. He wanted God to accept him on his terms.

**Ephesians 2:8-9** *For by grace are ye saved through faith; and that not of yourselves: It is the gift of God: not of works, lest any man should boast.*

## II.  He traded beauty for blood
God had an appointed period, appointed place, and an appointed process for these offerings according to verse three. Cain's offering was beautiful. His offering may have even cost more than Abel's offering. His offering may have involved more toil and labor than Abel's offering. The reason his

offering was rejected was because it was not what God said, and there was not one drop of blood in the entire offering. There is nothing beautiful about man and his sin. (Describe what the two altars looked like when they were done)

A. One altar was bloody, the other was beautiful.
B. One altar was received, the other was rejected.
C. One altar was pleasing, the other was proud.
D. One altar was worship, the other was works.
   (1 John 1:7, Exodus 12:13,1 Peter 1:18-19)

## III. <u>He traded trying for trusting</u>

He trusted his way and his works over God's way and God's Word. Cain would rather try than to trust!

False religion: Jude 11 calls it the Way of Cain!

False religion is marked by:

A. Force ...................................................Gen. 4:8
B. Falsehood .........................................Gen. 4:9
C. Futility.................................... Gen. 4:10-12
D. Fear .......................................... Gen. 4:13-15

***Conclusion:*** Rather than look to God he looked to himself. This is what apostasy teaches men to do is trust in their works rather than the work of Christ.

# "Cain the Angered"
## (The Wrath of Cain)
### Sermon #161

Text: Gen. 4:5-7

**5** *But unto Cain and to his offering he had not respect. And Cain was very wroth, and his countenance fell.* **6** *And the LORD said unto Cain, Why art thou wroth? and why is thy countenance fallen?* **7** *If thou doest well, shalt thou not be accepted? and if thou doest not well, sin lieth at the door. And unto thee shall be his desire, and thou shalt rule over him.*

Intro: I want us to deal tonight with an angry man. This man was not only an angry man but he is the first man in the Bible and in history to display a human driven by anger. (Apostasy leads to anger. Example: Muslims)

### *It's very clear to see that Cain had:*
1.   A hate problem. He hates God and his brother.
2.   A humility problem. He would not say he was wrong.
3.   A heart problem. His heart was not right with God.

### *Three things about the anger of Cain.*
1.   His anger is experienced. ................................ vs. 5
2.   His anger is expressed ..................................... vs. 5
3.   His anger is exposed ....................................... vs. 6
4.   His anger could have been extinguished ......... vs. 7

God gave him what he needed in this verse to overcome his anger.

**I.** <u>**He gave him his way - vs. 7**</u>
  A.   It is the right way.
  B.   It is the rewarding way.
  C.   It is the redeemer's way.

**II.** <u>**He gave him his warning - vs. 7**</u>
  A.   This warning was stern.
  B.   This warning was swift.
  C.   This warning was simple.

**III.** <u>**He gave him his word - vs. 7**</u>
  A.   This word was personal.
  B.   This word was promising.
  C.   This word was powerful.

**Proverbs 22:24** *Make no friendship with an angry man; and with a furious man thou shalt not go:*
**Proverbs 21:19** *It is better to dwell in the wilderness, than with a contentious and an angry woman.*
**Proverbs 14:17** *He that is soon angry dealeth foolishly: and a man of wicked devices is hated.*
**Ephesians 4:26** *Be ye angry, and sin not: let not the sun go down upon your wrath:*

<u>Look how anger affects a man.</u>

**I.** <u>**It affected his Lord - vs. 6**</u>
  A.   It displeased him.
  B.   It distanced him from him.

**II.** <u>**It affected his life - vs. 7**</u>
  A.   He is a mad man. (not thinking straight)

B.　He is a miserable man. (no happiness)

**III.　It affected his loved one - vs. 8**
　　A.　The innocent man suffers.
　　B.　The immediate family member suffers.

***Conclusion:*** Cain could have obeyed God but he was too prideful, too angry, and too jealous to do so. Anger is nothing more than a WORK OF THE FLESH.

**Colossians 3:8** *But now ye also put off all these; anger, wrath, malice, blasphemy, filthy communication out of your mouth.*
**James 1:20** *For the wrath of man worketh not the righteousness of God.*

# "Cain the Assassin
## (The Wickedness of Cain)
### Sermon #162

Text: Gen. 4:8-15

**8** *And Cain talked with Abel his brother: and it came to pass, when they were in the field, that Cain rose up against Abel his brother, and slew him.* **9** *And the LORD said unto Cain, Where is Abel thy brother? And he said, I know not: Am I my brother's keeper?* **10** *And he said, What hast thou done? the voice of thy brother's blood crieth unto me from the ground.* **11** *And now art thou cursed from the earth, which hath opened her mouth to receive thy brother's blood from thy hand;* **12** *When thou tillest the ground, it shall not henceforth yield unto thee her strength; a fugitive and a vagabond shalt thou be in the earth.* **13** *And Cain said unto the LORD, My punishment is greater than I can bear.* **14** *Behold, thou hast driven me out this day from the face of the earth; and from thy face shall I be hid; and I shall be a fugitive and a vagabond in the earth; and it shall come to pass, that every one that findeth me shall slay me.* **15** *And the LORD said unto him, Therefore whosoever slayeth Cain, vengeance shall be taken on him sevenfold. And the LORD set a mark upon Cain, lest any finding him should kill him.*

Intro: Cain's life is about to take a turn for the worse. He is about to carry out what has been building in his heart. If the sins of the heart are not dealt with, they eventually become sins of the flesh.

**I.   Cain's crime - vs. 8**
   A.   His crime was a crime of deception.
   B.   His crime was a crime of destruction.
   C.   His crime was a crime of death!
         He turns further away from both God and his brother. Those who loved him are the ones he hated. He had no reason other than the fact that his pride had blinded him.

**II.   Cain's creator - vs. 9-10**
   God is now having a second conversation with Cain. The first conversation was a warning but this is a witness. God is going to call out Cain's sin.
   A.   The Lord asked about his sibling in vs. 9
   B.   The Lord answers about his sibling in vs. 10
   C.   The Lord acknowledges his sin in vs. 10
         Cain shows nothing but deception and disrespect to his Creator in vs. 9 (met a man that got out in sin and was bitter at others because he is paying for his sin)

**III.   Cain's curse - vs. 11-12**
   Cain buries his brother like a seed in the ground. It was a seed of sin, and it is about to blossom before him.
   A.   God cursed what was precious to Cain.
   B.   God cursed what was prosperous to Cain.
         He simply cut his blessing off. Cain was only as good as God was willing to bless him.
   C.   God cursed what was pride to Cain.

He made a god out of the ground! The very ground he came from! It is safe to say he loved and lived for this world.

**IV.   Cain's complaint – vs. 13-15**
Verse thirteen is proof that man may not admit his sin, and he may not own up to his sin, but he will not get by with his sin. God is going to judge man for his sin.

What is sad is that Cain feared man more than he feared God in vs. 14.

Pride will cause man to be more concerned about what man thinks rather than what God thinks. Example: Coming to an altar.

### *Cain is a marked man in vs. 15*
A.   He marks his misery.
B.   He marks his madness.
C.   He marks his murder.

**Conclusion:** You cannot sin and not get scarred. As much as this was a mark of safety for Cain it was a mark of sin. Had he not sinned against God and his brother he would not have needed this mark. Can you imagine the embarrassment of having to explain this to your children and grandchildren.

# "Cain the Architect"
## (The Work of Cain)
### Sermon #163

Text: Gen. 4:16-24

**16** *And Cain went out from the presence of the LORD, and dwelt in the land of Nod, on the east of Eden.* **17** *And Cain knew his wife; and she conceived, and bare Enoch: and he builded a city, and called the name of the city, after the name of his son, Enoch.* **18** *And unto Enoch was born Irad: and Irad begat Mehujael: and Mehujael begat Methusael: and Methusael begat Lamech.* **19** *And Lamech took unto him two wives: the name of the one was Adah, and the name of the other Zillah.* **20** *And Adah bare Jabal: he was the father of such as dwell in tents, and of such as have cattle.* **21** *And his brother's name was Jubal: he was the father of all such as handle the harp and organ.* **22** *And Zillah, she also bare Tubalcain, an instructer of every artificer in brass and iron: and the sister of Tubalcain was Naamah.* **23** *And Lamech said unto his wives, Adah and Zillah, Hear my voice; ye wives of Lamech, hearken unto my speech: for I have slain a man to my wounding, and a young man to my hurt.* **24** *If Cain shall be avenged sevenfold, truly Lamech seventy and sevenfold.*

Intro: We have now come to the last sermon on the life of Cain. He is clearly an individual that has gone from bad to worse. His downfall began with disobedience, false pride. These led to anger, stubbornness, rebellion, and murder. God has confronted him, cursed him and marked him for his sin. Even after all this he could have found mercy if he would have only humbled himself and admitted he was wrong.

## *When we come to vs.16 we see:*
1. His Departure ................................. "He went out"
2. His Deterioration "From the presence of the Lord"
3. His Dwelling .............. "Dwelt in the Land of Nod"
   Nod means, "wandering". This dwelling place suggests that he was lost. Cain the first man ever born into life died lost. Cain knew where paradise was, saw the blood sacrifices, even participated in the ritual of worship, but never embraced the heritage that his daddy Adam had passed down to him. Just like a lot of people today.

## *In vs. 17 we see:*
1. Cain's companion
   The question has often been asked where did Cain get his wife? It's obvious that he either married a sister or niece. There was nothing sinful or shameful then because the commandment had not been given against marrying a near relative. In fact, God gave them a specific commandment to be fruitful and multiply and replenish the earth. That's the same commandment He gave Noah.
2. Cain's child
   His Child's name is, "Enoch". Enoch means, "to initiate, to dedicate, or to inaugurate". Now why would Cain Name his son Enoch?
3. Cain's city
   Like all false leaders he set out to build his own paradise where he would be his own god. Cain

names this city after his own son. He wants to be recognized, remembered he wants to leave a legacy behind.

## As we look at this city we will see that it had:
1.  Great Social activity.... (People are moving into it)
2.  Great Secular activity............(Lots of opportunity)
3.  Great Scientific activity ........ (Lots of discoveries)
4.  Great Sinful activity.

## This is the first "Sin city" ever built.
1.  This city had no God.
2.  This city had no government.
3.  This city had no guidelines.
    Man goes in 4 chapters from a garden to a city and his situation only gets worse. Cain determined that if he could not have a garden then he would have a city. Let's look at Cain the architect and see the work of Cain.

## I. The men of this city - vs. 18, 21-22
In the bible an individual's name could reflect their character or the circumstances surrounding their birth or childhood.

Enoch - vs. 18 .initiated, dedicated, or inaugurated
Irad - vs. 18 ........................... fugitive or a wild ass
Mehujael - vs. 18 ...........................smitten of God
Methusael - vs. 18 ...................man who is of God
Lamech - vs. 18.....powerful, conqueror, wild man
Jabal - vs. 20 ........................... to flow, to produce
Jubal - vs. 21 ........................... to flow, to produce
Tubal-Cain - vs. 22 ................. to flow, to produce

Not any of these men ever showed any interest in the things of God. These were the leaders of the city and they were just like their founder, lost and living for earthly pleasures. Is this not the society we live in today?

II. **The morals of this city - vs. 19**

There were no morals. This verse tells that these men were immoral men. They did what was right in their own eyes. Lamech was a polygamist.

His first wife's name is Adah, which means, "ornamental". She represents the lust of the eye.

His second wife's name was Zillah, which means, "shade or seductress". She represents the lust of the flesh. The lust of the eye, the lust of the flesh and the pride of life had gotten the men and the morals of this city.

III. **The monetary gain of this city - vs. 20-22**

Lamech's boys were all three very successful business men. This no doubt made him a very powerful and wealthy man.

A. Jabal was successful in tents and cattle
.............................................................. vs. 20

B. Jubal was successful in harps and organs
.............................................................. vs. 21

C. Tubal-Cain was successful in brass and iron
.............................................................. vs. 22

    1. The first son brought economics to this city.

    2. The second son brought entertainment to the city.

3.   The third son brought engineering to the city.
     This city was booming in every worldly way possible.

## IV.   The music in this city - vs. 21

Not adding anything to the text, but you know that the music they were playing and singing was not to glorify the Lord. Nothing about this city was to the glory of God.

A.   This music was worldly music.

B.   This music was wicked music. (No morals)

## V.   The metals in this city - vs. 22

The word "brass" is also the same word for the word, "copper". Tubal-Cain had a sister Naamah whose name means: "Pleasant or lovely". This third lady mentioned in our text could represent the pride of life in Lamech life. Having her last and later in life could have brought complete and total pride to Lamech. This is picturing him as a very worldly man, with worldly ambitions and business.

A.   Jabal's success represents prosperity.... vs. 20

B.   Jubal's success represents pleasure ...... vs. 21

C.   Tubal-Cain's success represents power vs. 22

D.   Lamech was seen as a man of power. There is another Lamech in Chapter 5:28. He was also a powerful man. His power was not of this world but of God.

## VI.  The murder in this city - vs. 23-24)

This city was built by a murderer, and we see that it continues. Lamech suggests in vs. 23 that he should be more protected by God than Cain himself, because he claims it was done in self-defense. Will God forgive a murderer? Sure He will, but he must confess his sin and guilt before God. It's interesting that Lamech makes no attempt to talk spiritual until he commits an awful crime. He gets spiritual for one reason because he fears for his life. Men and women often start thinking on a spiritual level when they are facing life threatening or life changing matters.

## VII.  The memory of this city - vs. 25

Most of the men in chapter five are recorded at least twice. Not these men. There is no memory of this city. Heaven shows no interest in them because they showed no interest in heaven. They lived lost and they died lost. In chapter 5 the Bible emphasizes that those godly men lived! (vs. 3, 5, 7, 9, 10, 12, 13, 15, 16, 18, 21, 25, 26, 28, 30) Those men that lived for God are forever remembered.

*Conclusion:* This city is a mark of what the last days are going to be like just before Jesus comes! The world will be just as it was in chapter 4. Cities with no God, no government, and no guidelines! Social and spiritual decline, scientific development, some devotion but lots of sinful activity! Then in chapter five just as Enoch is raptured out before the flood, the church is going to be raptured out before the tribulation! The Lord will have

53

the Jews safe in the ark as He did Noah and when the judgement is passed we come back to earth like Noah did with a better promise of a better day! And oh what a city God will have built, one better than the first ever built! Not a sin city but a Holy city!

# "How to Murder Your Brother!"
## Sermon #164

Text: Gen. 4:8

**8** *And Cain talked with Abel his brother: and it came to pass, when they were in the field, that Cain rose up against Abel his brother, and slew him.*

Intro: I want us to focus on the first murder in the Bible. It's interesting that the first death in the bible was not carried out by God but by man. This brings Romans 6:23 to life. The shocking scene is one of a brother killing his own brother. You would expect it to be anyone other than two brothers involved. My question is what motivated Cain to kill his own brother?

1. **Cain was a famous man**
   Everyone in the world literally knew who Cain was. Even today if you say, Cain and Abel" the world still knows who and what you are talking about.
2. **Cain was a fiery man**
   It did not take much to set him off. If a man will argue and be disrespectful toward God, then he will do the same toward man.
3. **Cain was a fighting man**
   He was willing to take matters into his own hands. He was willing to fight his own brother to get what he wanted out of life.
4. **Cain was a fruitful man**
   His life had been blessed. God had been good to him. He was very proud and saw his blessings as

success in life. He felt as though he had accomplished something great. He wanted everyone including God Himself to feel as he did about his accomplishments. Cain forgot who it was that blessed the seed in the ground. He forgot who gave him the strength, who sent the sunshine, and who sent the rain.

**5.** **Cain was a faith man**

Cain has two conversations with God in this chapter. He was not an atheist. Cain had participated in worship and even brings an offering himself to God. Faith is good if it's in the right person. Faith in oneself or ability will always crumble. Cain was a man of faith and this sin happened under the form of religion. It all started at a worship service.

**6.** **Cain was the first man**

Everyone knew he was the older brother. Cain was the first man. According to the last phrase of vs. 7 the Lord assures Cain if he does right he will be accepted. He tells him that Abel will still have a desire to look up to him and that he will keep the first born birth right. Cain was so jealous that he could not stand the very thought of his brother being more blessed than him or his brother being first. Cain was not going to obey God but he was not going to be second either.

Our text tells us how Cain carried out his mission. This verse tells us how Cain murdered his own brother.

**1 John 3:15** *Whosoever hateth his brother is a murderer: and ye know that no murderer hath eternal life abiding in him.*

### I. <u>He used friendly talk</u>
"And Cain talked with Abel"
He came to Abel and communed with him as though nothing was wrong. Abel thought this was nothing more than a casual conversation.

### II. <u>He used family ties</u>
"Abel his brother"
The fact that he was Abel's brother gave him the advantage. He knew Abel would not have his guard up. He knew that Abel would trust him because he was his brother.

### III. <u>He used fulfilled time</u>
"And it came to pass"
Meaning he waited for the right moment to attack him. He wanted to catch him off guard. He wanted to get him alone so he could have the advantage over him. He knew that timing was everything.

### IV. <u>He used familiar territory</u>
"When they were in the field"
These boys were totally different in their occupations. They were different in their spirits and their spirituality. The only thing they had in common was the field. They both went to the field everyday. Even though they were in different fields

of service, Cain knew the field was where he needed to launch his attack.

## V.    **He used a fleshly tactic**
"Cain rose up against Abel"

A.    He was stronger
Cain knew that Abel was the weaker brother and sought to take advantage of it. He murdered him because he could.

B.    He was strategic
He calculated every move in his mind. He planned the attack. He went behind his brothers back and destroyed him.

***Conclusion:*** This happens in our pulpits among preachers. This happens in our pews amongst the people. One of the greats sins today is the sin of murdering your brother.

# "There is Someone Bigger Than You in This Room!"
## Sermon #165

Text: 1 Kings 17:1

**1** *And Elijah the Tishbite, who was of the inhabitants of Gilead, said unto Ahab, As the LORD God of Israel liveth, before whom I stand, there shall not be dew nor rain these years, but according to my word.*

Intro: Our text gives us an introduction into the life and ministry of Elijah. However, I do not want to focus that much on Elijah, but I want us to look at King Ahab. I want us by way of introduction to consider three things concerning the life of King Ahab.

I.     **Ahab and his status - vs. 1**
      A.     Ahab was big..............................He was king
      B.     Ahab was bad............. He was a wicked king
             Chap. 16
      C.     Ahab was boss...... He was the final authority

II.    **Ahab and his sinfulness - 1 Kings 16:33**
      A.     His sin was a religious sin.
      B.     His sin was a rebellious sin.

III.   **Ahab and his surprise - vs. 1**
Elijah steps on the scene out of nowhere. He has a sermon for King Ahab. This sermon is short, stern, and surprising! Note the phrase in your Bible "Before whom I stand". Elijah wants Ahab to know

that he is not standing before him, but that there is someone bigger than him in the room.

**(Title)**

A.   He is bigger than Ahab in his wealth.
B.   He is bigger than Ahab in his wisdom.
     (Won't out smart God!)
C.   He is bigger than Ahab in his warfare.

Many face the same problem today that Ahab faced. Pride, prestige, popularity, pleasures and possessions have blinded them to the point that they think they can do whatever they want.
If you look closely at the message Elijah preached to Ahab, you will see that it was:

1.   An individual message............... "Said unto Ahab"
2.   An inspiring message........."the Lord God of Israel liveth"
3.   An intense message........."There shall NOT be dew nor rain"

Ahab makes an awful mistake in our text. He never saw anyone but Elijah. He saw the man but not the message. Ahab you can't see that there is someone bigger than you in the room. Some people can't see past the preacher!

**I.   <u>There is no response in our text</u>**
     Ahab does not say one word in our text. It's almost as if he pays Elijah's sermon no mind at all. He hears it but he doesn't respond to it. Sounds like

60

people today. Most come to hear preaching and that is as far as they intend on going with it. We should come to both hear and respond to what God speaks to us about.

***Illustration:*** Church I preached in and no one came one night. Went back 5 years later and preached and no one came.

## II.  <u>There is no repentance in our text</u>
If only Ahab would have repented! God would have been merciful and forgiven him. He shows no remorse and he shows no repentance in our text. Repentance is a must with God! He could have cried, confessed, committed to God. He chose not to.

***Illustration:*** Young woman in sin who lifted her head in an invitation and shook it no at me. Her life has fallen apart.

## III.  <u>There is no remedy in our text</u>
The message of Elijah offered Ahab no remedy. No repentance then no remedy! Just as Ahab walked away from Elijah, God walked away from Ahab. Lives could have been saved, revival could have been brought to the people of God. One man's sin brought judgement on an entire nation. Ahab received no invitation to get right with God. If Ahab would have fallen on his face, then God would have granted him and the nation mercy.

***Conclusion:*** Just as one man's sin shut up the heavens, hindered the dew and rain from falling and caused many to suffer, so it is in the church. Why is there no spiritual dew nor rain in our churches today? Sin hinders God's showers of blessings. Recognize that there is someone bigger than you in this room. Look past the man and see the message.

# "The Man God Chooses to Use"
## Sermon #166

Text: 1 Kings 17:1
**1** *And Elijah the Tishbite, who was of the inhabitants of Gilead, said unto Ahab, As the LORD God of Israel liveth, before whom I stand, there shall not be dew nor rain these years, but according to my word.*

Intro: This morning we focused on Ahab. Tonight we want to focus on Elijah. **(Title)** There are many interesting things in our text concerning the man God chose to use.

1. **When Elijah started - vs. 1**
   There is very little to be said about this place. Some say Tishbite means "reformer". Other say it has to do with the place of his residence or birth. God chose a man of whom there is little to be spoken about. One reason is because it's not about the man, it's about the message. We know nothing of his parents, his childhood or his poverty.

2. **Where Elijah stayed - vs. 1**
   Gilead was a rough and rugged territory, east of Jordan. Gilead was divided between the tribes of Gad and Manasseh. It is likely that he pertained to either Gad or Manasseh. It was known for its thick forest and wild beasts. The people who lived there, lived in rural houses in little villages, tents and huts. It was wilderness territory.

3.  **Who Elijah saw - vs. 1**

    Elijah was a man on a mission to see the king. He did not send word by a servant or a prophet. He marched in himself and spoke directly to the king.

4.  **What Elijah said - vs. 1**

    Elijah wanted Ahab to know that his God was alive. He did not come in the name of some dead god. His God was, "the Lord God of Israel that liveth."

5.  **Why Elijah spoke - vs. 1**

    Of everything found in this verse, this is what amazes me the most. Elijah spoke with such courage, confidence, and conviction. When he closed his message, notice what he said... "according to my word." Notice he didn't say according to thy word, but my word.

This is an important part of this verse. This tell us not only what Elijah said but why Elijah could speak. It was his word! This little phrase proves why God used Elijah to be his man.

To go further back in Elijah's ministry, you have to go to the N.T. not the O.T. 1 Kings 17 is as far back as we can study Elijah in the O.T. However, James takes back a little further and tells us what Elijah was doing before he went into Ahab's presence. This wasn't the first time Elijah had been in the presence of a king. (James 5:17) God just answered his prayer!

# Three truths about the man God chose to use.

**I.  Elijah was buried - vs. 1**

God had him deep in the shadows of the forest. We can always rest assure that God always has a man somewhere in the shadows. A true man of God ready to come forth and deliver the message of the hour. God chooses men in obscure places just like he did Elijah. To be used of God, you have to be willing to be buried, to be hid, to be in the shadows. (Examples: Moses 40 years in the desert, JESUS 30 years as a carpenter)

**II.  Elijah was bold - vs. 1**

Elijah was not apologetic about the message. He did not water it down for the King. He didn't try to dress it up or try to make it sound good. Ahab had the power to take his head off! Elijah was strong in the Lord. In this verse Elijah tells Ahab that Jehovah is Living, (as the Lord God liveth) Jehovah is Lord, (before whom I stand) Jehovah is his life, (The name Elijah means "Jehovah is my strength".) The Lord stood with him because he stood for the Lord. If Elijah had waited for some fellow man to go with him he would have never have gone.

**III.  Elijah was burdened - vs. 1**

The reason God chose Elijah was because Elijah chose God. Elijah got so burdened that he started praying, "God shut the heavens up and let there be no rain or dew" God told him one day his prayer had been heard. God said to Elijah go and tell Ahab there will be no rain nor dew theses years according to your word.

IV. **Elijah was Balanced**
This was a Biblical prayer according to Duet. 11:17, Moses told Israel that if they turned aside and worshiped other gods and served them; He would shut up the Heaven, that there should be no rain. Elijah no doubt prayed according to the words of Moses.

***Conclusion:*** God always uses the man that makes himself available. It's often been said that God is not looking for ability but availability. How true this is. Elijah just made himself available, and God used him greatly.

# "Finding Something Better
# Than the Brook!"
Sermon #167

Text: 1 Kings 17:2-7

**2** *And the word of the LORD came unto him, saying,* **3** *Get thee hence, and turn thee eastward, and hide thyself by the brook Cherith, that is before Jordan.* **4** *And it shall be, that thou shalt drink of the brook; and I have commanded the ravens to feed thee there.* **5** *So he went and did according unto the word of the LORD: for he went and dwelt by the brook Cherith, that is before Jordan.* **6** *And the ravens brought him bread and flesh in the morning, and bread and flesh in the evening; and he drank of the brook.* **7** *And it came to pass after a while, that the brook dried up, because there had been no rain in the land.*

Intro: Elijah comes on the scene in verse one with authority, with an announcement, and with an assurance that only comes from God. It is because of his confrontation with Ahab that three distinctive things happen in his life. All three of these were sovereign acts of grace by God.

1.      Elijah hears from God......................................vs. 2
2.      Elijah is hidden by God .................................vs. 3
3.      Elijah is helped by God..................................vs. 4

All of this happens at special place in Elijah's life. God had a promise, God had a place, and God had provision for Elijah. That place was the brook! Do you realize that once God mentions the word brook in vs. 3 He doesn't stop talking about it the rest of this story? The brook is mentioned in every single verse.

Vs. 3 ................ The brook was reserved for Elijah.
Vs. 4 ................ The brook was running for Elijah.
Vs. 5 ................ The brook was residing for Elijah.
Vs. 6 ............. The brook was refreshing for Elijah.
Vs. 7 ................. The brook was retired for Elijah.

1.    There's miracles by the brook.
2.    There's meat by the brook.
3.    There's a message by the brook.

1.    The brook represents God's protection.
2.    The brook represents God's providence.
3.    The brook represents God's provision.

Elijah learned how to make it through the dry seasons of life by the brook! The brook was a great experience in Elijah's life. Everybody would like to have a brook experience! (You may have had one in your lifetime.)

Wait just a minute! One day I was reading this text and the Lord spoke to me and said Elijah found something better than the brook! You might ask what did he find better than the brook? (Vs. 2, 8) While I believe we have unusual experiences with the Lord from time to time, most days appear to be ordinary. It's not every day that we can have brook experiences. But long before Elijah had the brook, he had the book! "The word of the Lord".

1.    Just as Elijah stayed by the brook, he stayed by the book!
2.    Just as Elijah sat by the brook, he also sat by the book.
3.    Just as he supped by the brook, Elijah supped by the book.

But there is a vast difference between the brook and the book! Look at vs. 7-8 The brook dries up but not the book! The book is still fresh, still flowing, still for all who will seek it and receive it.

1.    It's a Divine Book...........................................vs. 2
2.    It's a Directed Book .......................................vs. 2
3.    It's a Different Book.....................................vs. 3-4
4.    It's a Dependable Book ................................vs. 5-6
5.    It's a Diligent Book ......................................vs. 7-8

*__Conclusion:__* Who needs the brook when you got the book! You want to know why Elijah did not shout over the brook, nor did he pout over the brook when it dried up! He had the book! We can't always have the brooks but we can always have the book! The brook was earthly; the book is spiritual. The brook was temporary; the book is eternal. The brook was an extra-ordinary experience; the book is an every day experience. Friend don't spend your days looking for unusual brook experiences. We know that God in His wisdom will send those experiences when He sees it necessary. Spend your days looking at something better. Have a book experience every day of your life. Sit by the book and listen and learn what God has for you that day. Elijah was simply following orders in our text. This is what you and I need to do is follow the instruction the Lord has for us each and every day.

# "What You Can Learn from Two Old Birds
## Sermon #168

Text: 1 Kings 17:2-7

**2** *And the word of the LORD came unto him, saying,* **3** *Get thee hence, and turn thee eastward, and hide thyself by the brook Cherith, that is before Jordan.* **4** *And it shall be, that thou shalt drink of the brook; and I have commanded the ravens to feed thee there.* **5** *So he went and did according unto the word of the LORD: for he went and dwelt by the brook Cherith, that is before Jordan.* **6** *And the ravens brought him bread and flesh in the morning, and bread and flesh in the evening; and he drank of the brook.* **7** *And it came to pass after a while, that the brook dried up, because there had been no rain in the land.*

Intro: Tonight I want to draw our attention to the birds in our text. These birds are mentioned two times in our text. Now we don't know exactly how many there were, but for the sake of argument we do know that there were at least two. We are going to watch these birds as they serve both their Creator and mankind. We as Christians have the same responsibilities as they did. You might wonder, why preach on two old birds? How could their lives make a difference? I mean what could you possibly learn from a couple of old birds?
**(Title)**

I.  **Their flight - vs. 4**
    A.  They've been given a mission. (I have commanded)

71

B.   They've been given a ministry. (to feed thee)
C.   They've been given a map. (feed thee there)
They did not volunteer but they were called upon by their Creator.

## II.   Their favor - vs. 4
A.   They found favor as they were used.
B.   They found favor as they were unified.
C.   They found favor as they were unclean.
Leviticus 11:15; Duet. 14:14, says that these birds are unclean and an abomination!
These birds not only found favor but they also showed favor. Those who experience grace will know how to show grace on others as well. This is grace for grace.
1.   They showed grace in their going.
2.   They showed grace in their giving.

## III.   Their food - vs. 6
A.   Bread and Flesh was a provision for Elijah.
B.   Bread and Flesh was a promise for Elijah.
C.   Bread and Flesh was a picture for Elijah. (Christ)
D.   Bread and Flesh was power for Elijah. (Strength)

## IV.   Their Faithfulness - vs. 6
A.   They were faithful at the early dawn. (Morning)
B.   They were faithful at the end of the day. (Evening)

**_Conclusion:_** These birds were faithful to the task given to them and so should we be. Just as He feeds all in the next story, He feeds all in this story. God took care of them also. God has used His creation many times to teach man the lessons of life. After all we are all a part of His creation. We were once announced unclean and an abomination in the site of God. Through His mercy and grace He forgave our sins and used us not because of us, He used us in spite of us. He allows us to have a part in His service to others who are in need.

# "The Dry Brooks of Life"
## Sermon #169

Text: 1 Kings 17:2-7
**2** *And the word of the LORD came unto him, saying,* **3** *Get thee hence, and turn thee eastward, and hide thyself by the brook Cherith, that is before Jordan.* **4** *And it shall be, that thou shalt drink of the brook; and I have commanded the ravens to feed thee there.* **5** *So he went and did according unto the word of the LORD: for he went and dwelt by the brook Cherith, that is before Jordan.* **6** *And the ravens brought him bread and flesh in the morning, and bread and flesh in the evening; and he drank of the brook.* **7** *And it came to pass after a while, that the brook dried up, because there had been no rain in the land.*

Intro: In this passage we have examined the book, examined the birds, now let's examine the brook. There is the description of the brook. (vs. 3) The very name, "Cherith" means drought telling us it usually dries up faster than others.

### Three opinions of where people think Cherith is:
1.   Some place it on the eastern side of Jordan, supposing it was one of the "wadys" of Gilead.

2.   Others believe it was one of the brooks which ran into Jordan on the western side, of those some prefer the "wady" Faseal or the "wady" Kelt.

3.   Others believe it to be in the valley Cherith.

No doubt, wherever Cherith lies, it was a very rough terrain. This valley is one of the wildest ravines in the wide region. In some places it is at least 500 ft. deep, with dark thickets and limestone banks covered with caves in which Elijah may have lived concealed from Ahab, by a brook that was known to be of a drought even in the good times.

1.  **There is the drinking from the brook - vs. 4**
    It's a miracle within itself that he enjoyed water when there was no rain. Only God could do that. Every drink he took was a reminder of how good God had been, is being, and would continue to be in his life.

2.  **The dwelling by the brook - vs. 5**
    Elijah was able to experience cool water, a cool breeze, and a cool place to rest his head in the hard times of life. God had given him an oasis in the desert for his obedience and refreshment. Though it was bad times for many, it had become brook times for Elijah.

3.  **The dining by the brook - vs. 6**
    God not only gave him water but he gave him bread and flesh in the morning and in the evening. These were added blessings in his life. (Ephes. 3:20) The Lord didn't just get him by but he took good care of him.

4.  **The drying up of the brook - vs. 7**
    Why would God allow this brook to dry up?

1. To teach us not to trust in the blessings but the one who gives the blessing.
2. To loosen our roots, in case to move us to some other location in life or service.
3. To remind us that earthly brooks, no matter how needed or good, cannot compare to the eternal river that flows from a throne, that never runs dry.
4. Because Elijah had to feel the effects of the sermon that he was preaching.

## Four truths about the dry books of life.

### I.    It was given
Elijah could have spent his time complaining about the brook drying up but he doesn't. After all he didn't deserve the brook but God had given him one. Instead of complaining about it drying up he thanked God for the time it was brought into his life. You can spend your days complaining about everything that has dried up in your life or you can spend your days thanking God for the provision He has given you.

### II.   It was gradual
He didn't wake up one day and it was gone. God allowed him to see what He was doing a little at a time. He could literally see the stream getting smaller by the day. He knew he was running out of water. This allowed Elijah to prepare himself for what God would do next in his life. Where God would take him and what He would have him do.

III. **It was God**

He didn't know what God was doing, but he knew He was doing something. He knew that as sure as God gave the brook, he knew God was drying it up. This meant God had not forgotten him but that He was still working in his life. God is as much at work in our lives in drying things up as He is in sending things into our lives.

IV. **It was good**

When Elijah left the dry brook, he knew God had done a good thing in his life. He was also convinced that this now meant He had something better ahead. That God was now going to work in a different way. He knew that if God dried up the brook then that meant he didn't need the brook. The dry brook was the best thing for Elijah. We know that God had more provision for him as He did for others.

***Conclusion:*** Vs. 7 "and it came to pass" meaning it was fulfilled, also, "after a while" represents a year often in scripture. We must remember that the Lord's timing is everything. He may test us at times, but He is never tested. He knows exactly what He is doing. Even when what we have enjoyed and what has sustained us is taken away, rest assure that God has another plan. He has a better plan that will prove perfect in our lives.

# "How to Find Faith in Your Famine"
### Sermon #170

1 Kings 17:8-16

**8** *And the word of the LORD came unto him, saying,* **9** *Arise, get thee to Zarephath, which belongeth to Zidon, and dwell there: behold, I have commanded a widow woman there to sustain thee.* **10** *So he arose and went to Zarephath. And when he came to the gate of the city, behold, the widow woman was there gathering of sticks: and he called to her, and said, Fetch me, I pray thee, a little water in a vessel, that I may drink.* **11** *And as she was going to fetch it, he called to her, and said, Bring me, I pray thee, a morsel of bread in thine hand.* **12** *And she said, As the LORD thy God liveth, I have not a cake, but an handful of meal in a barrel, and a little oil in a cruse: and, behold, I am gathering two sticks, that I may go in and dress it for me and my son, that we may eat it, and die.* **13** *And Elijah said unto her, Fear not; go and do as thou hast said: but make me thereof a little cake first, and bring it unto me, and after make for thee and for thy son.* **14** *For thus saith the LORD God of Israel, The barrel of meal shall not waste, neither shall the cruse of oil fail, until the day that the LORD sendeth rain upon the earth.* **15** *And she went and did according to the saying of Elijah: and she, and he, and her house, did eat many days.* **16** *And the barrel of meal wasted not, neither did the cruse of oil fail, according to the word of the LORD, which he spake by Elijah.*

78

Intro: The story of Elijah and this widow is a very encouraging story in the Bible. However, nothing can be more important in this story than the timing of it.

1.   These were some very hard times.
2.   These were some very hungry times.
3.   These were some very humble times.
4.   These were some very holy times.

Just because things get hard doesn't mean they can't be holy. The good news is that God is still at work in the famine or the hard times of life. Just because some of us may give up doesn't mean He does.

1.   This widow has a little boy.
2.   This widow has very little bread.
3.   This widow has very little belief.

She's not planning on making it thru the famine. She plans on dying in the hard times of life. Sounds like a lot of people today. She is losing faith. This is the primary reason God is sending Elijah to her. He is not interested in performing another miracle. He is interested in rescuing someone's faith!

1.   God know she has to keep going.
2.   God knows she has to keep giving.
3.   God knows she has to keep gathering, or she will lose faith.

She has everything she needs to make it thru this famine. The problem is she just can't see it because the famine has hindered her faith. We allow famines to hinder our faith. She is allowing what's happening around her physically to affect her spiritually. She has her eyes off her creator and on her circumstances and she is losing faith fast.

So God is going to send her a preacher! God didn't move Elijah to feed him, he was already doing a good job of that by the brook. Also the Lord could have fed her without Elijah. (In fact one more mouth to feed was the last thing she needed. But God wants to feed her faith.) So he sends her a preacher! Someone stronger in faith than what she was. Don't you appreciate the Lord sending stronger saints into your life?

1.  Elijah has seen the miracle.
2.  Elijah has tasted he meat.
3.  Elijah has tasted the bread.
4.  Elijah has been given orders by God.

God is going to use him to show her she has what she needs to make it through the famine or the hard times of life. He comes to the gate of the city in verse ten and meets her. Elijah faces as much of a test as anyone in our story. He doesn't know who she is, what she looks like, or where she lives. This wasn't the only widow woman there I'm sure. So he has to meet the right one. He uses spiritual words when speaking to this woman. He is looking for faith as well. Had she passed him by, he would have kept on searching. In vs. 10-11 he uses the word "pray". I know it can mean "ask" but "pray" is a spiritual word, "pray" is a faith word. He's trying to help her faith in this famine. God is wanting her to see she has what she needs to make it through. (1 Jn.5:4)

**I.** **She has the right inspiration in the famine - vs. 9**
God is speaking to this woman. He had already spoke to her before He spoke to Elijah. She had heard from God but was having trouble believing God.

**II.** **She has the right instruction in the famine - vs. 9**
He clearly had told her what he wanted her to do. Sustain a preacher. She does not believe she can do this. She is looking at the circumstances around her. The resources that she has are not sufficient for what God has asked her to do. If God commands us to do something, then He will give us the resources to do it.

**III.** **She has the right ingredients for the famine - vs 12**
   A.   She has water. (Word)
   B.   She has meal. (Christ)
   C.   She has oil. (Spirit)

**IV.** **She has the right instruments for the famine - vs. 12**
   A.   She has barrel. (Container-Christian)
   B.   She has a cruise (Container-Christian)
   C.   She has two sticks (Cross)
   D.   She has fire. (Judgement bread that gives life)

Faith always brings Christ into an individual's life. What this lady needed was Christ. The Lord Jesus Christ was all she needed and he was typified all around her.

**V.**   <u>**She has the wrong intentions in this famine – vs. 12**</u>

    A.    She is depressed ...................................... vs. 12
            Up to this point this woman has said nothing. God has spoken to her, Elijah has spoken to her, but she has said nothing. She has lost her husband, and she has lost hope.

    B.    She is doubting ...................................... vs. 12
            When this woman begins to speak she calls God, Elijah's God not her God. (thy God) Being a gentile she most likely thought all gods were the same. She really doesn't know if Elijah is a true prophet or a false prophet at this point.

    C.    She is depleted ...................................... vs. 12
            When she does start to speak, listen to how she speaks. She says, "I have not a cake, but a handful, a little cruse". There is no faith in her vocabulary. She knows what God has said and she knows what Elijah needs but she does not have much faith in either.

    D.    She is defeated ...................................... vs. 12
            The only thing she believes is that she and her son are going to die. She has already witnessed this and now she is waiting for this come to pass.

There is only one thing that will help build faith; that's another word from God. How do we get more faith? We must get more word in us. (Rom.10:17) God will use His man to deliver His word. That is exactly what Elijah is about to do in vs. 13.

Now getting this woman to do what has been asked is not as hard as getting her to believe in what she is doing. We have a lot of people not doing and a lot of people doing but not believing in what they are doing.

She is given a command in verse nine to go get some water. She exercises a measure of faith in verses 10-11 in fetching this water. Even though she is wanting herself, she is still willing to go get and give some water in the hardest of times. We see here a measure of faith.

She goes from hearing a commanding word in vs. 9 to a continual word in vs. 13. I'm glad the word of the Lord will come a second time. There is no shortage of His word in the famines of life. I want us to focus on the word she is receiving in vs. 13-14

1.  A word of comfort. "Fear not"
2.  A word of confirmation. "Go and do as thou hast said"
3.  A word of challenge. "But... make me.... a little... first"
4.  A word of connection. "And after make for thee"
5.  A word of compassion. vs. 14

The Lord does not leave her wondering any longer but tells her what will happen if she obeys.

***Conclusion:*** Even when she could not see, did not understand, and did not fully believe, she obeyed the Lord's command.

1.  She is exercising her faith in vs. 15 (went & did)
2.  She is enjoying her faith in vs. 15 (at every meal)
3.  She is experiencing her faith in vs. 16

Faith must first be exercised before faith can be enjoyed. Each day was a step of faith but it got a little bit easier. She could trust God today in her famine all because she had trusted him the day before.

# "A Soul Stirring Revival"
## Sermon #171

Text: 1 Kings 17:17-24

*17 And it came to pass after these things, that the son of the woman, the mistress of the house, fell sick; and his sickness was so sore, that there was no breath left in him. 18 And she said unto Elijah, What have I to do with thee, O thou man of God? art thou come unto me to call my sin to remembrance, and to slay my son? 19 And he said unto her, Give me thy son. And he took him out of her bosom, and carried him up into a loft, where he abode, and laid him upon his own bed. 20 And he cried unto the LORD, and said, O LORD my God, hast thou also brought evil upon the widow with whom I sojourn, by slaying her son? 21 And he stretched himself upon the child three times, and cried unto the LORD, and said, O LORD my God, I pray thee, let this child's soul come into him again. 22 And the LORD heard the voice of Elijah; and the soul of the child came into him again, and he revived. 23 And Elijah took the child, and brought him down out of the chamber into the house, and delivered him unto his mother: and Elijah said, See, thy son liveth. 24 And the woman said to Elijah, Now by this I know that thou art a man of God, and that the word of the LORD in thy mouth is truth.*

Intro: I want us to begin by looking at three key thoughts found in verse seventeen.

1.    The timing of this text. "And it came to pass"

2. The trouble in this text. "son of the women…fell sick"
3. The tragedy in this text. "there was no breath left in"

This widow's life goes from bad to worse in our story. She comes though this famine and now she is facing a whole different problem in her life. The thing she feared the most has come upon her but not in the same way nor at the same time she thought it would. Elijah takes this young man up into the loft and he is revived. Note with me what vs. 22 says.
1. This revival was a spiritual revival. (His soul)
2. This revival was a physical revival.

**(Title)**

I want us to focus on two words in vs. 22. The words "soul" and the word "revived". I'm interested in what this soul-stirring revival brought into their lives.

## Everybody in this house can use revival.
1. Elijah needed revival because he was doing.
2. The woman needed revival because she was doubtful.
3. The boy needed revival because he was dead.

## Here are 7 things this soul stirring revival brought her.

## I.    The remembrance of her sin - vs. 18

This woman obviously has had a past. She knew that Elijah was not afraid to call out an individual's sin for he did Ahab's in vs.1. Thank God for preachers that will preach on sin and not care about who is in the congregation or who is guilty. In order to have revival we must be willing to remember our sin. Most individuals want to forget it and act like it doesn't exist.

## II.     The releasing of her son - vs. 19
Elijah takes her burden and makes it his own. Had he not, this woman would have sat there and died with the boy. Her burden would have killed her. A lot of folks sit in church so burdened down, and it is draining the life out of them both physically and spiritually.

## III.    The request for her sorrow - vs. 20
Elijah does not know what God is doing in her life, but he is going to seek the Lord on her behalf. Elijah wanted to be praying right for her. He did not want to ask God to do something if she was being punished, so he prayed about her sin. We should pray in a detailed manner for people when they are burdened down. This is important in order to see our prayers answered for them.

## IV.    The returning for her in supplication - vs. 21
Once Elijah hears no rebuke from the Lord, he proceeds to pray for his request. The Lord's silence was as much an answer as if He had spoken. The Lord did not call out this woman's sin so Elijah

accepted the fact that He was not judging her. (Silence can be a very loud answer at times.) His prayer is not victorious the first time, not the second time, but it is the third time. We must be willing to be steadfast in prayer.

## V.   The reviving of her son - vs. 22
Persistent prayer pays off and the Lord revives her son. Is there someone you need to see the Lord revive? Be persistent if you want to see life in them again. Don't quit praying for them.

## VI.   The revealing of her son - vs. 23
Elijah carries the boy away from her as a heavy burden. Elijah now carries the boy to her as a holy blessing! He wanted her to see that prayer changes people's lives.

## VII.   The renewing of her spiritually - vs. 24
There is a greater resurrection in this passage! The boy comes alive physically but in vs. 24 the woman comes alive spiritually! Up until this point this woman has not said one spiritual thing. Even after the meal barrel she has not glorified God. In fact, this may have happened simply because her faith was still not complete. She announces in this verse why God did what He did. She learned about grace in the barrel and truth in her son! She learns in the famine her preacher could preach. Now she learns in the death of her son her preacher can pray.

Elijah was a preacher, a man of prayer, and a man of power. (vs. 24) God has revealed to this woman that both His word and His prophet are true! The assurance was worth the agony!

**_Conclusion:_** It took a son to be born, to live, to die, and to rise again for her faith to be complete. When she saw the risen son she fully believed. The same is still true for sinners today. Faith in the risen Son is complete faith!

# "God Sees the Big Picture"
### Sermon #172

Text: Luke 4:25-26
**25** *But I tell you of a truth, many widows were in Israel in the days of Elias, when the heaven was shut up three years and six months, when great famine was throughout all the land;* **26** *But unto none of them was Elias sent, save unto Sarepta, a city of Sidon, unto a woman that was a widow.*

Intro: Jesus has just announced His earthly ministry in the synagogue at Nazareth. His family and friends do not accept His ministry but rather they reject His ministry. Our Lord then begins to teach them the importance of not rejecting Him. In doing so, one of the illustrations He uses is the story found in 1 Kings 17. Jesus is about to tell them the truth, the whole truth and nothing but the truth.

"But I tell you of a truth..." This phrase amazes me because the last word the widow spoke of in 1 Kings 17 was about truth. She surfaces again in the N.T. and the very embodiment of truth is speaking about the truth concerning her life.

1. This woman is famished ................................ vs. 25
2. This woman is far away ................................ vs. 25
3. This woman is forsaken ................................ vs. 25
4. This woman is found .................................... vs. 26
5. This woman is famous ............................. vs. 25-26

## Christ speaks in our text about:

***Conclusion:*** This woman lived her life, facing these hardships never really knowing fully why they came upon her. God did not reveal everything to her. She could not see all that He was doing in her life. The same is true in our lives. We face hardships but do not fully understand the plan of God. We can't always see why God even allowed such difficulties in our lives. The truth is that God sees the big picture. One of the reasons this widow went through what she did in 1 Kings 17 was to be an example for our Lord to use many years later. Christ used her to be an illustration of Israel's rejection of Him and how that in grace He would turn to the Gentiles. I'm not sure if this widow woman was present to hear when Christ spoke these words or not. However, I can't help but to think that somewhere down the way, she learned that the hardships she faced in one dispensation, was so she could be a tool for the Savior to use in another dispensation. We never know how and when God is going to choose to use our lives. He sees the big picture!

# "The Many Things That Trouble Us in the Ministry"
## Sermon #173

Text: Luke 10:38-42

**38** *Now it came to pass, as they went, that he entered into a certain village: and a certain woman named Martha received him into her house.* **39** *And she had a sister called Mary, which also sat at Jesus' feet, and heard his word.* **40** *But Martha was cumbered about much serving, and came to him, and said, Lord, dost thou not care that my sister hath left me to serve alone? bid her therefore that she help me.* **41** *And Jesus answered and said unto her, Martha, Martha, thou art careful and troubled about many things:* **42** *But one thing is needful: and Mary hath chosen that good part, which shall not be taken away from her.*

Intro: Our story is centered around Jesus and the two sisters of Lazarus. This is a family that He loved and was very close with. He often loved to visit with them in their home. I want Christ to feel the same about me and my family. I want Him to feel the same welcome and desire to visit in my home.

This passage takes place in late December at the time of the Feast of Dedication. Lazarus is probably in Jerusalem for the feast. Christ will be crucified next spring at the Feast of Passover. Jesus visits their home in Bethany on the Mount of Olives near Jerusalem.

Notice the first character mentioned in this family is Martha. (vs. 38) Martha's name appears four times in our text. Martha is known for her ability to work and to serve others. We certainly need Marthas today. I want us to notice four things about Martha this morning.

**(Title)**

1. Martha and her house..................................vs. 38
2. Martha and her hospitality ..........................vs. 38
3. Martha and her haste..................................vs. 40
4. Martha and her hindrances..........................vs. 41

Now I'm sure there were things that she was troubled about that are not in the text. There were things that only she and those that were present could see she was troubled about. There were things that only Martha and Mary could see that she was troubled about. There were things that only Martha and Jesus could see that she was troubled about. (vs. 41 say, "thou art careful and troubled about many things")

Martha is not just troubled, but Jesus said she is "careful and troubled about many things." The word careful means "to be drawn in many directions". Sometimes we find ourselves just like Martha in life. Martha is troubled about many things concerning her ministry. She is ministering to Jesus and to others for Jesus. The tragedy is that she is doing it all while troubled in the ministry. There are three things in vs. 40 that we can see that she was troubled about while ministering for and to Jesus. The same three can trouble us if we are not careful.

# I. She is troubled about her service - vs. 40

A. Service caused her to be extremely busy ....... ..................................................... vs 40

B. Service caused her to be extremely burdened................................................ vs. 40

C. Service caused her to be extremely bothered................................................ vs. 40

We must constantly be focused on who we serve, why we serve, and when we serve. If we lose sight of these truths, we will become troubled about our service. Service then becomes a burden instead of a blessing. (Col. 3:23-24)

# II. She is troubled about her Savior - vs. 40

A. She approached him.

B. She accused him.

C. She answered him.

When Martha came to Jesus she interrupted his conversation to question Him about this matter of service. Martha felt confident that she had the answer on how to get more service done. How many times have we been so troubled about getting the job done that we responded the same way Martha did? She wants Jesus to respond more aggressively to others in this matter of service.

# III. She is troubled about her sister - vs. 40

A. Mary had disappointed Martha.

B. Mary had deserted Martha. (So she thought.)

Martha had become so troubled about the ministry that day that she had allowed serving Jesus to divide her and her sister. She was more concerned about what Mary was not doing rather than what she was doing. Is not the goal of serving Jesus to get others closer to Him? To get others around him? Martha had helped to accomplish this but had failed to do so herself.

**Conclusion:** The problem wasn't Mary; the problem was Martha. Martha wasn't doing a bad thing. She was doing a good thing with a bad spirit. How many times have we become troubled, drawn in many directions while serving Jesus and serving others for Jesus? We must remember that it is not all about the ministry it is about all about the man.

# "The Good Part of Serving Jesus"
### Sermon #174

Text: Luke 10:38-42

**38** *Now it came to pass, as they went, that he entered into a certain village: and a certain woman named Martha received him into her house.* **39** *And she had a sister called Mary, which also sat at Jesus' feet, and heard his word.* **40** *But Martha was cumbered about much serving, and came to him, and said, Lord, dost thou not care that my sister hath left me to serve alone? bid her therefore that she help me.* **41** *And Jesus answered and said unto her, Martha, Martha, thou art careful and troubled about many things:* **42** *But one thing is needful: and Mary hath chosen that good part, which shall not be taken away from her.*

Intro: I know that in reality that every part of serving Jesus is good. However, our Lord makes it clear that there is a part that stands alone from all others. That is the part that I want to preach on today. **(Title)** We want to focus on Mary in our text tonight.

1.  Mary is in a lovely place..........................(at Jesus)
2.  Mary is in a lowly place....................(at Jesus feet)
3.  Mary is in a listening place.......... (heard his word)
4.  Mary is in a learning place.......(learning the word)

This is the place that Jesus said in vs. 42 was the "good part." My question is why is this the good part. The Bible is going to tell us in this passage.

**I.    Because it is a near place - vs. 39**
   A.    He encourages to come and fellowship.
   B.    He enjoys us when we fellowship.
   C.    He enables us to come and fellowship.

**II.    Because it is a neglected place - vs. 40**
   A.    Many are too busy.
   B.    Many are too burdened.
   C.    Many are too backsliden.

**III.    Because it is a needful place - vs. 42**
   A.    We need this part daily.
   B.    We need this part desperately.

**IV.    Because it is a nice place - 42**
   A.    There is sweet fellowship.
   B.    There is sweet favor.
   C.    There is sweet forgiveness.

**V.    Because it is a now place - vs. 42**
   A.    We don't have to wait to get in His presence.
   B.    We don't have to wonder if we can get in His presence.
   C.    We don't have work to get in His presence.

***Conclusion***: If you take this part out of serving Jesus then you know what we become. We become slaves instead of servants. If there is no relationship, then we have missed God's plan for our lives as Christians. He wants us to serve Him because we love Him.

# "Dealing With the Deep Places of Life"
### Sermon #175

Text: Ps. 130:1-8

*1 Out of the depths have I cried unto thee, O LORD. 2 Lord, hear my voice: let thine ears be attentive to the voice of my supplications. 3 If thou, LORD, shouldest mark iniquities, O Lord, who shall stand? 4 But there is forgiveness with thee, that thou mayest be feared. 5 I wait for the LORD, my soul doth wait, and in his word do I hope. 6 My soul waiteth for the Lord more than they that watch for the morning: I say, more than they that watch for the morning. 7 Let Israel hope in the LORD: for with the LORD there is mercy, and with him is plenteous redemption. 8 And he shall redeem Israel from all his iniquities.*

Intro: This Psalm is the sixth of the seven penitential Psalms. Psalm one hundred thirty is very unique because of:

1. **Its Primary Association**
   Some believe it to be a psalm of David or "like David" which would give authorship probably to that of Hezekiah.

2. **Its Prophetic Anticipation**
   Like in many of the psalms, the psalmist is pointing us to the fulfilment of Israel's Day of Atonement.

### 3.   It's Personal Application

This Psalm is known as the Pauline Psalm of the O.T. The entire human race is in the depths of sin and the only way out is to cry out to God and find forgiveness. We know that man cannot save himself, so Jehovah must save him.

I want to zero in on the first phrase of this Psalm. The Psalmist says, "Out of the depths". *The Hebrew meaning for being "in the depths" refers specifically to being caught in a dangerous and deep waters.* This image occurs many places in the O.T. (Is.51:10, Ezek. 27:34) but none is more powerful than Psalm 69:1-2. This gives us a clear image of what the writer meant when he said, "Out of the depths". Life has a lot of deep places in it. Sometimes out of nowhere we find ourselves in those dangerous and deep waters.

*Those deep waters may be the depths of:*
1.   Despair
2.   Disappointment
3.   Discouragement
4.   Depression
5.   Disgrace

A deep place in life can be anything that seems to overwhelm or overtake you. It is a situation where one feels as if they are drowning in despair. It could be anything from emotional anxiety, mental stress, financial struggle, physical ailment, to spiritual issues.

The Psalmist takes the time to tell us that his situation was more than just a single struggle. He says, "Out of the **depths**." Why would he want to talk about the deep places of life? We all know that they are dark, dangerous, and desolate places. We all feel insecure and as if our life is going to be taken at any moment. We feel abandoned by man and sometimes even by God. ***However, Deep places produce deep devotion. Diamonds sparkle in the dimness.*** We must learn to deal with the deep places of life. I want us to look at what the Psalmist learned from the depths of this life.

**(Title)**

**I.**  **He learned more about prayer - vs. 1-2**
  A.  The tears of prayer .................................. vs. 1
  B.  The travail of prayer............................... vs. 2
  C.  The triumph of prayer ............................ vs. 2
It took a deep place in life for him to learn of this. Depth usually silences all that it engulfs. The deep places of life could not silence prayer. Under the floods, prayer lived on. Above the roar of the billows, faith arose. It doesn't really matter we are in life if we can pray. Prayer is never more real that when it rises out of the worst places. (Charles Spurgeon)

**II.**  **He learned more about pardon - vs. 3-4**
  A.  A simple fact ............................................ vs. 3
      (We are all guilty)
  B.   A sure forgiveness................................. vs. 4
  C.  A sudden fear .......................................... vs. 4

Our Lord keeps a record but he does not act upon that record. Our record has and will remain forgiven.

**III.** **He learned more about patience - vs. 5-6**
    A.    Patience in waiting.................................vs. 5
    B.    Patience in his word ..............................vs. 5
    C.    Patience in watching .............................vs. 6
Waiting is beneficial because it tries our faith, exercises our patience, trains us in submission, and helps us to appreciate the blessing when it comes.

**IV.** **He learned more about promise - vs. 7**
    A.    This is a national promise .................(Israel)
    B.    This is a near promise .........(soon to happen)

**V.** **He learned more about pity - vs. 7**
    A.    This pity is powerful ............. (with the Lord)
    B.    This pity is present........................ "there is"
    C.    This pity is precious.........(Unlike any other)
We are not comforted by what is within us but by what is within our God.

**VI.** **He learned more about purchase - vs. 7-8**
    A.    Redemption is plenteous........................vs. 7
    B.    Redemption is promised ........................vs. 8
    C.    Redemption is perfect ...........................vs. 8
            (leaves nothing undone, but completes us now and forever.) The psalmist was looking out of the depths to the promise of a coming redeemer. We are looking out of the depths the promise of a King!

***Conclusion:*** The fact is that the Psalmist may have known of these things but he now has a deeper knowledge of them because of the deep places of life. He had been to the depths of despair but to the depths of prayer. He had been to the depths of life, but not alone, he had been there with God his father.

Made in the USA
Columbia, SC
17 March 2019